I0111860

CORRECTIVE JUDGMENT

The Program of God For Us

For My Parents
Louis and Evelyn Goldstein
My Daughter, Maria
My Granddaughters, Sarina & Juliette

Copyright © 2015 by Living Epistles Ministries
All rights reserved under International Copyright Law.
Published @ Long Island, NY March, 2015

ISBN: 13: 978-0692402672
ISBN: 10: 0692402675

Corrective Judgment
Sheila R. Vitale

No part of this book may be reproduced, in any form,
without written permission from the publisher

Requests for permission to reproduce selections
from this book should be mailed to:

Living Epistles Ministries
Sheila R. Vitale
P O Box 562
Port Jefferson Station, NY 11776-0562 USA
(631) 331-1493

Living Epistles Ministries

~ Judeo-Christian Spiritual Philosophy ~
Sheila R. Vitale
Pastor, Teacher, Founder
PO Box 562
Port Jefferson Station, NY 11776 USA

CORRECTIVE JUDGMENT

The Program of God For Us

Edited and Adapted as a Book by
Sheila R. Vitale

CORRECTIVE JUDGMENT

The Program of God For Us

Is an Adaptation of an Excerpt from
CCK Message #667, Honor, Integrity & the Character of God,
Which Was Transcribed and Edited For
Clarity, Continuity of Thought, And Punctuation by
The *LEM* Transcribing and Editing Team

Living Epistles Ministries

~ Judeo-Christian Spiritual Philosophy ~

Sheila R. Vitale

Pastor, Teacher & Founder

Ministry Staff

Anthony Milton, Teacher (South Carolina)
Brooke Paige, Teacher (New York)
Sandra Aldrich (MN) (July 7, 1975 – April 18, 2021)

Administrative Staff

Susan Panebianco, Office Manager

Editorial Staff

Rose Herczeg, Editor

Technical Staff

Lape Mobolaji-Lawal, Database Administrator

Ministry Illustrators

Cecilia H. Bryant (Oct. 18, 1921 – Oct. 23, 2013)
Fidelis Onwubueke

Music Staff

June Eble, Singer, Lyricist and Clarinetist
(July 20, 1931 – Jan. 24, 2024)
Don Gervais, Singer, Lyricist and Guitarist
Rita L. Rora, Singer, Lyricist and Guitarist

Table of Contents

The Alternate Translation Bible©

The Alternate Translation Bible (ATB)
Is an original interpretation of the Scripture that
Is not intended to replace traditional translations.

Alternate Translation of the Old Testament©
Alternate Translation, Exodus, Chapter 32
   (Crime of the Calf)©
Alternate Translation, Daniel, Chapter 8©
Alternate Translation, Daniel, Chapter 11©
Alternate Translation, Genesis 9:18-27
   (The Noah Chronicles, Second Edition) ©

Alternate Translation of the New Testament©
Alternate Translation, 2 Thessalonians, Chapter 2
   (Sophia)©
Alternate Translation, 1st John, Chapter 5©
Alternate Translation, the Book of Colossians
   (To The Church At Colosse) ©
Alternate Translation, the Book of Ephesians
   (To The Church At Ephesus) ©
Alternate Translation, the Book of Corinthians, Chapter 11
     Corinthian Confusion) ©
Alternate Translation, the Book of Jude
   (The Common Salvation)©

Alternate Translation of the Book of the Revelation of
    Jesus Christ to St. John©
Traducción Alternada del Libro de Revelación de Jesucristo©

CORRECTIVE JUDGMENT
The Program of God for Us

INTRODUCTION

Corrective judgment raises Christ from the dead. I am talking about the resurrection of Christ in the individual, and His ascension above the powers and principalities that hold the mind and body captive. That is what the program of God is all about.

The program of God is salvation, deliverance, and the ascension of Christ in the individual to 'meet the Lord in the air'. There is a rapture, but it is a spiritual rapture. Christ, the awakened Abel, has to rise above the Serpent's household, which is Cain, Leviathan and Satan, and as soon as He ascends above, He has to bring them into submission. He has to break their power. We might say He has to kill them.

The powers and principalities that rule mankind have to die to their authority and become subjects of Christ in the individual.

Sheila R. Vitale

WHO ARE WE?

We are the personality, and the personality is attached to the body. The personality grows out of the body. Fallen Adam is incarnating and producing these bodies and personalities as clothing for the fallen soul in this world. Initially, when we come into this world, we are the animal skins that Jehovah gave to Adam and the Woman by a power beyond human reproduction. There is a spiritual power that causes us to be born. Some women are barren. Some men are infertile and do not produce sperm, or their sperm count is low, or for whatever reason, they cannot impregnate a woman or fertilize an egg. Barrenness is a reality. This means there are certain conditions that produce a human being, and if those conditions are not met, the human beings are not produced; they are not born. Everyone is not guaranteed a child, although most people can have one. It is not a given, it is not absolute. There are powers and conditions that influence human reproduction.

Eternal life exists in the spiritual (supernal} worlds and everything that they unify with receives eternal life. Adam the living soul, separated from the life-giving powers in the world above, died and fell down into this world. The spiritual powers of this world that control human reproduction are the parts of the fallen soul that survived Adam's fall.

Adam's brain was severed from his spinal cord and he died completely. His head was resurrected in the person of Jesus of Nazareth, but He is a quadriplegic to the degree that the Church has not yet yielded up the use of their bodies to Him. Brethren, who can understand the depths of it?! Compared to God we are as ignorant as an ant is to us, so He gives us spiritual truth in parables.

The Lord Jesus Christ, to whatever degree we can understand it, is the resurrected head of Adam, the spiritual man who died, but His body, the Church, is a quadriplegic. We are the body of the rectified Adam in the person of the Lord Jesus Christ who is limited because of us. Only His brain is fully rectified. We are His body in this world that limits His ability to walk when He wants to walk, or stand up when He wants to stand up, or throw a ball when He wants to throw a ball. Our bodies do not obey Him because we (the spinal cord) are separated from Him (the brain). This is a metaphor, brethren, to let us know that the Lord Jesus Christ is working feverishly to reconnect His brain to His spinal cord.

The spinal cord is a single cord that flows through the vertebral column or spinal column, which consists of many separate bones or vertebrae. The vertebral, or spinal column, encloses the spinal cord. Each of us is a bone or a vertebra in the spinal column. The spinal cord can be likened to the spirit of God that joins us all, and each one of us is a vertebra or a bone, or a soul, that surrounds that spinal cord to form the spinal column.

The fallen soul (the spinal cord that is disconnected from the brain) is the power that causes incarnation in our present human (animal) form (we are mammals). As a result of that disconnect, it has become evil.

Immortality, the supernal worlds, and righteousness co-exist, and cannot be separated. So, when a soul separates from its union with the supernal worlds, it separates from eternal life and from righteousness.

The prophet, Malachi, says that God loved Jacob and hated Esau, but God does not hate like man hates, and God does not love like man loves. We also read in the Scripture that Isaac loved Esau, and Rebecca loved Jacob. The father loved one son, and the mother loved the other son. Does this mean that Rebecca did not love her son, Esau? No. It means that Rebecca had a rapport with her son Jacob.

In most instances, parents that have two or more children have more of a rapport with one child than with the other(s). It does not mean that they do not love their other children. Maybe one child is like the mother and one child is like the father. Each parent has a rapport with the child that is more like him or herself, and that commonality increases when the child becomes an adult. It does not mean they do not love their other children.

Love is an action word. Love is something that you do. You love all of your children by being equally fair to each of them. You may have more of a rapport with one of your children. You may have more in common, more of the same desires and interests in life, with one child than with the other(s), but when it comes to making out your will, love says that you give to each child equally. Love is doing right by everyone.

My mother used to say, ***Where did you come from?*** She did not know where I came from because I was not like her at all. The truth is that I am spiritually and emotionally like my father's family. Mothers may expect or hope to be best friends with their daughters, but I had absolutely nothing whatsoever in common with my mother. The daughter that she had a rapport with was my sister, Sandy. They were like two peas in a pod. They were the same. Does that mean that my mother did not love me? No. My mother did the best she could for me, and she was fair. She was a fair person.

When the Scripture says that Rebecca loved Jacob and Isaac loved Esau, it means that each parent had a rapport with one or the other child. Following this understanding, we can say that God loves the people that He has something in common with, who have the same interests that He has. What interests God? He is interested is in ***us***, the people of spiritual Israel who are accomplishing His plan for the salvation of the nations. He hates people that are not interested in Him or

His Word. He hates people that are not interested in the salvation of the world, but He does not hate like a man hates.

The word *hate* is the inaccurate translation of a Hebrew word that means that God does not have much in common with people who are not interested in knowing Him. If you do not have much in common with somebody, you spend less time with them. That is what the word *hate* means when it is applied to God. *Hate* is an unfortunate choice of the King James translators, because it makes the God of Israel look bad.

Every human being born of a woman has the opportunity to be loved by God in accordance with this understanding of love. How do you become loved by God? You get interested in what He is interested in.

This is not an unusual principle in human society. Married women who find that they are growing apart from their husbands, especially after they have had children (because the woman is all bound up raising the children and the man is all bound up in his job and hobbies) are usually advised to get interested in what their husband is interested in. I am talking about life, and this is what life is all about.

THE RESURRECTION OF CHRIST IN US

The Core of the Scripture

What is the core principle of the Scripture, the most important idea? It is the resurrection of Christ. What does that mean?

There is a supernal world where eternal life exists and there is this fallen world where death covers everyone that is born into it. A residue, a drop of life from the supernal world is in all of us, but that drop of life is dead. How can a drop of life be dead? The dead drop in fallen mankind is the potential of the human race to be renewed and resurrected.

Jesus of Nazareth, the first mortal man to experience renewal and resurrection, became Jesus, the Christ, the head of the body of a people who are destined to have the same experience. He also became a permanent resident of the world above and, through a relationship with Him, all of mankind now has the opportunity to be joined to that eternal place.

Our dead drop is our only potential to experience true life. If it remains alone, unmarried, it cannot do anything (Jn 12:24). Just like an egg in the ovum of a woman must wait for the sperm that will actuate its potential, the dead drop in the midst of mankind awaits the seed of the Lord Jesus Christ, the catalyst that produces spiritual renewal and resurrection.

The resurrection of Christ is the precursor. That must happen first, before the head is permanently reconnected to the spinal cord of the body. There has to be something in the skins of mankind for the supernal life of the upper worlds to join to. The head is not joining to a dead seed. It is joining to an awakened, or an enlivened, or a quickened seed. That drop of life that is in all of us is a seed that has to be quickened, made alive by the grafted Christ (Js 1:21), the resurrected head in each of is. It has to war against, overcome and completely crush every ungodly thing that surrounds it. It has to come to a place where it can say, jo*in with me*. It is like a barren woman going to the doctor, or Rachel, saying to Jacob, *give me a child or I will die*, and Jacob saying, *Am I God?*

The plan of salvation is to reconnect the fallen soul of mankind to the supernal worlds. The problem is that when the fallen soul separated from life, immortality and righteousness, it became death, mortality, and evil. After the separation and polarization of the head and the spinal column, what had been a singularity of immortality, righteousness, and life, became a plurality of opposing powers, of which only one can survive. The fallen soul of mankind is so morally opposite the righteous, spiritual man that she is destined to marry, that she would not survive their union.

The plan is not to destroy the evil powers, because before the evil powers fell, they were a part of the supernal world. There was a singularity of righteousness, life and immortality that was bisected. Immortality, life and righteousness continues to exist in the world above but, now, mortality, death and evil possess the lower worlds.

I preached that mortality, death, and evil had to be destroyed for a long time, but today I envision a better solution. No, they do not have to be destroyed. They must be overcome. They must be brought into submission to righteousness and re-integrated into the immortal world where eternal life exists.

There is no place in God's Kingdom, however, for the destructive mind and tormenting emotions that are found in fallen mankind today. They are spiritually perverse, and must be swallowed up by the resurrected Christ.

6

Those of us (which is all of us) who are a part of death, mortality and evil today must experience a change of character because, even the best of us, does not have the character of the glorified Jesus Christ. It is impossible to rise to the level of morality required to receive eternal life apart from Him (1 Cor 1:30).

We, the personality and the body, are projected images, or skins, that cover the fallen soul and fallen spinal cord that exist in a spiritual plane. We, the personality and the body, are of the earth. The fallen soul presses on the earth and molds it and we pop out into this world. That is the spiritual explanation of our physical birth. The explanation for the existence of this world is that a spiritual woman became pregnant, and this world, the environment of her spiritual baby, came into existence.

An infant lacks self-control. It cannot control its bowel movements; it cannot control its bladder. It cannot control whether it cries or not. It cannot control its arm and leg movement. We have a baby that is completely out of control, but inside of him is a drop of the supernal world that is completely paralyzed. This is the situation.

It takes a lifetime of learning to control ourselves and, ultimately, as we become adults, to learn to choose between good and evil. As we are educated spiritually, we learn to choose Christ. We are to choose the thoughts and the impulses and the desires of Christ over the thoughts and the impulses and the desires of that physical baby that has now become a physical adult. Some people grow up and their mind is disciplined enough. Some people are not at all disciplined and do not have any self-control. There are also varying degrees in-between.

However, the plan is to re-join every single one of us to the supernal worlds, but this can only happen if we overcome the impulses, thoughts, desires, and inclinations of the flesh, the physical body, and the carnal mind, and choose Christ.

THE AWAKENING OF ABEL

We cannot be re-connected to the supernal worlds before Abel is awakened in us. What awakens Abel in us? It is not likely that Abel is awakened before He is exposed to the spiritual power of God through His Word or through His Spirit, in one way or another. It could be as a young child your parents take you to an anointed Church, and the anointing awakens Abel in you. The dead drop is called Abel. His name changes to ***Christ***, the anointed one of God, when the flesh of ***Jesus Christ, is grafted*** to him.

When he is dead, he is the same as the powers and principalities that incarnated him in this world of death. He is a part of the Serpent's household. When he is dead, he is one of them. He has to be awakened to who he really is, a drop, a seed of the supernal world, isolated, trapped inside this box of a human body, with no hope of ruling over the Serpent's household, unless and until a relative, his big brother, rescues him.

That principle is in the Scripture, Jesus is our big brother. What does that mean? Abel in us has no hope of overcoming the inclinations of the Serpent's household, which is the carnal mind and the physical body, until a relative of the supernal worlds joins him to strengthen Him. What does a ***relative*** mean? It means someone from above who is of the same spirit, or Christ in another person. God is rescuing that seed of Himself in the Israel of God.

Paul taught us that not everyone that is born a physical Jew, is a Jew or Israelite.

Romans 2:28-29
    ²⁸ FOR HE IS NOT A JEW, WHICH IS ONE OUTWARDLY;
NEITHER *IS THAT* CIRCUMCISION, WHICH IS OUTWARD IN THE
FLESH:
    ²⁹ BUT HE *IS* A JEW, WHICH IS ONE INWARDLY; AND
CIRCUMCISION *IS THAT* OF THE HEART, IN THE SPIRIT, *AND*
NOT IN THE LETTER; WHOSE PRAISE *IS* NOT OF MEN, BUT
OF GOD. **KJV**

Romans 9:6
    ⁶ NOT AS THOUGH THE WORD OF GOD HATH TAKEN
NONE EFFECT. FOR THEY *ARE* NOT ALL ISRAEL, WHICH ARE
OF ISRAEL: **KJV**

If you are reading this, you are probably an Israelite. We are talking about the Israel of God (Gal 6:16), meaning the seed in a human being that comes from God, no matter what your ethnic background. There may be more spiritual Israelites coming from a particular ethnic background, but it does not matter. You could be an Israelite from your ancestry, and not know it. Ten of the 12 tribes have lost their tribal identification, and there have been many inter-marriages. On the other hand, you may not have any physical Israelites in your ancestry. You may be a spiritual Israelite if Abel, the dead drop in you, has been awakened and transformed by the grafted Christ.

The proof of who you are is your response to the Spirit of God. The Scriptures talk about *the elect*. Jesus said, ***Let whosoever will, come***, but there has to be something in you that responds to the call. If there is something in you that responds to the call, you are the elect, and an Israelite.

The plan is that Jesus, the head, who is now immortal, should be re-joined to spiritual Israel, the Israel of God in the earth, and then, eventually, immortality, salvation, and deliverance from the evils of this world, is to be brought to the whole planet.

The first step is that Abel, who is born dead in us, is awakened. Abel is dead, meaning he died to the conscious awareness that he is related to God. He thinks that he is a part of the Serpent's household, but he is a drop of the supernal worlds. The Jewish teachers would call him *the Shekinah that went into captivity with Israel*.

He is a drop of God, but he lost his identity and is in complete agreement with Cain, Satan and Leviathan. He thinks he is one of them. Therefore, his God-consciousness has to be awakened, and re-educated. He has to be fed *the Doctrine of Christ,* which is his food. It is not enough to wake him up. A baby can die if he is not fed. His food is *the Doctrine of Christ*.

When Christ is grafted to Abel, he becomes powerful enough to throw off Cain, Satan, and Leviathan who are lying on top of him. It is as if the Lord Jesus Christ (who is in charge of this whole program) makes a judgment that Abel is now old enough and mature enough to overthrow them. Once Abel rises to the surface through union with Christ, he must rule over the powers and principalities in his mind and the lusts of the flesh.

THE WARFARE

Overcoming Our Carnal Mind

It is all about overcoming, and our job down here is to overcome. When we start overcoming, at this point we are no longer just a personality that is a projection of the fallen soul. When we start resisting the inclination of our fallen nature and the body, especially when we are doing it as a result of this understanding, we are now joining ourselves to Christ, and we are more than the personality that arises out of the body. We are in the process of being bonded to Christ.

As we mature (there is a maturation of the personality, a n d a maturation of the soul), the personality must choose between Christ and the carnal mind. The choice does not become evident to us until we are spiritually matured to some degree, and this understanding is imparted to us. It is the mindset that the personality chooses, or marries, as Paul says, that determines who we are. We have to choose one or the other. If we do not choose Christ, we default to the carnal mind.

We must overcome to be Christ. If we do not fight, we default to the carnal mind. This means our personality comes into agreement with our carnal mind. The personality must agree with either the carnal mind or the Christ mind. If we do not choose, we default to the carnal mind. If we choose Christ and start to resist the inclinations of our fallen nature, we can say that we are Christ. We are not the Lord Jesus Christ, but we, in our nature, are in the process of becoming Christ.

We are not yet born spiritually, even though we are born physically, and it is not yet determined who we shall be (1 Jn 3:2). The personality, which is female, must choose between the two males. To choose Christ is a battle, let me tell

13

you. However, you and the Lord are a majority. You can do it and you *will* do it.

It is all about the warfare that ensues once a personality chooses Christ, because Cain, Leviathan, and Satan seek to destroy that choice. The evil inclination will beat up the personality to loosen its grip on Christ through the typical pressures of life, such as a dying mother or loved one, the loss of a child, betrayal by a loved one, or a loss of finances.

Any tragedy known to humanity can be a pressure. The vicissitudes of life, up and down, up and down, weaken the individual personality that is hanging on to Christ, and strengthen Satan and Leviathan and, sometimes, the personality loses its grip on Christ.

THE POWER OF REPENTANCE

Should you lose your grip on Christ, there is no condemnation, just get back. You can get back. There is nothing that can separate you from God except your own sin. There is nothing outside of yourself that can separate you from God. There is no mistake that you can make, no sin that you can fall into, that Jesus will not forgive if you just come back to the Lord, repent, and ask for restoration, The Lord will surely restore you.

Restoration may or may not be instant, but He will take you back. There is nothing, no expression of the power of God within man that is more powerful than repentance. The power of repentance breaks the power of all judgments and decrees against you. I am not talking about curses coming from carnally minded people. I am talking about judgments and decrees from God. Decrees come down from God. There was a decree of death on my life. The sowing and reaping judgment that comes from God was killing me at 10 years old, but the Lord Jesus saved me from it somewhere

I will briefly tell you my story again. At the time the Lord called me, I had a dream. I was on this endless line, it was outdoors. The people were all filing before this big desk. It reminds me of the desk that the Supreme Court justices sit behind. It was very high. I could see the figure of a man sitting behind the desk, but I could not see his face. I did not know why I was there, but my turn before the judge came and he said, ***It has been decided that you should live.*** Then he picked up his gavel, banged it on the desk, and here I am.

It is real brethren, it is real. The courts of God are real. The government of God is real, and decrees go out, judgments go out as to who will live and who will die. What is going on in this country and Europe today, where there are human beings sitting on death panels, deciding who is to be denied medical treatment because they are too old, is all an attempt to emulate God.

Man wants to be God, but man cannot do what God does. Man has no right to decide who will live and who will die, but God has the right to decide who will live and who will die, and He does. ***God decides who will live and who will die***.

Repentance can break any decree or death sentence that comes from God, and certainly those that come from man. There is nothing available to us that is more powerful than true repentance. Confession of sin and saying, ***I am sorry*** is not the end of the matter of sin. True repentance comes from your heart. It begins with confessing that you did something wrong, and weeping about it. True repentance is about being so contrite that it brings you to tears, that you sorrow unto repentance, not unto condemnation. You must be truly sorry for what you have done - not because of the negative consequences, not because you are on your way to jail - but because you are convicted that you did something wrong.

There is nothing in the universe that can disannul the reality of that depth of repentance. There is no accusation from the accuser. Satan cannot stand against true repentance. We read about the court of God in the Book of Zechariah, where we see Joshua being tried. He is in filthy garments. He is in his humanity and the accuser and the Angel of the Lord are both there.

Zechariah 3:1-4
[1] AND HE SHEWED ME JOSHUA THE HIGH PRIEST STANDING BEFORE THE ANGEL OF THE LORD, AND SATAN STANDING AT HIS RIGHT HAND TO RESIST HIM.
[2] AND THE LORD SAID UNTO SATAN, THE LORD REBUKE THEE, O SATAN; EVEN THE LORD THAT HATH

CHOSEN JERUSALEM REBUKE THEE: *IS* NOT THIS A BRAND PLUCKED OUT OF THE FIRE?

³ NOW JOSHUA WAS CLOTHED WITH FILTHY GARMENTS, AND STOOD BEFORE THE ANGEL.

⁴ AND HE ANSWERED AND SPAKE UNTO THOSE THAT STOOD BEFORE HIM, SAYING, TAKE AWAY THE FILTHY GARMENTS FROM HIM. AND UNTO HIM HE SAID, BEHOLD, I HAVE CAUSED THINE INIQUITY TO PASS FROM THEE, AND I WILL CLOTHE THEE WITH CHANGE OF RAIMENT. **KJV**

There is an accuser in this world. There is an angel that goes before God, especially when you are serving Him. There is an angel that goes before God, just like in the book of Job, and says, *Look at that one over there. You think that one is Your servant? You think that o n e is Your preacher? You think that one is the one that honors You? Look at what they just did.* The challenge is to a righteous God, and He says, *If they did that, My law says this is the judgment on them. They should die for that.*

There are legitimate decrees and judgments that go forth from the supernal realms. This is not fantasy. We are all guilty! We are all guilty of one thing or the other and the Lord wants to bring us to repentance. God helps us by moving on our behalf to bring you to repentance. He does not remove the accusation because we answer an altar call, or say that we are sorry.

Our condition must change, Your condition and my condition must change. I cannot take back the sin that I committed. I wish I could. There are a lot of things I have done that I wish I could erase, but I cannot. I did them, whatever I did. I am human just like you are. It is done. But true repentance breaks the power of the decree that can bring great destruction into your life.

How does God bring us to repentance? Sometimes, the powers and principalities within us are too strong for Abel to rise above. Most of the time, they are too strong for the young Christ in us to rise above.

As I said previously, when your personality is trying to hold on to Christ, Satan and Leviathan beat up on you in the form of the pressures of life to try to make you let go of Christ. The reverse, or something similar, is true with God. The Lord pounds on the principalities in you that are pressuring you to let go of Christ. The Lord is beating on the principalities that are trying to make you let go of Him.

When this happens, the personality gets caught between the pressures of the carnal mind, and the pressures that Christ within them is putting on their evil inclination. The personality gets confused as to which side is God, and which side is the enemy. The greater the pressure, the more likely the person will let go. But if we do let go, the only thing that matters is that we make it back.

Once Christ is grafted to us, the Lord will fight for us from his engrafted position. He is not be willing to lose you because now, since His Son is quickened in you, he is fighting for His Son. But the truth is, He does, however, let the people that Christ is not grafted to walk away He lets some people walk away, and others He fights for.

The Lord has shown me that, most of the brethren do not understand what I have preached until it happens to them. I preach it, and I preach it, and I preach it, but it does not get through to them until they experience it.

JUDGING OUR SIN NATURE

You must be judging your sin nature at the same time that you swallow down the spiritual doctrine that you learn here or Cain will walk away with it. The Lord simply will not permit you to remain here if you are swallowing down this doctrine and not adequately judging your sin nature, because you would become evil. You would stand up on the evil side.

Maybe some people listening to me or reading this book have not been adequately dealing with their sin nature. The issue is this. I can only do what the Lord tells me to do, and even if I tell you about one of your character flaws, there is no guarantee which way it will go. It may help you, and it may not, especially if your reaction is to get mad at me. But telling you is the only thing I can do. All of my power is in my tongue, to tell you the truth. However, if your heart is right towards God, He will be there to help you.

When it is time for your sins to be exposed, God will call for a showdown with your sin nature. If you are really doing the best that you can and it is not enough, or you think you are judging your sins deeply, but God says you are not, He will call for a showdown. He will put pressure on you. He will force the warfare between Christ in you and your fallen nature.

You cannot sit in these meetings unless you also deal with your sins. If you do not, there will be an explosion. It is as simple as that. There is the easy way to go and there is the hard way, but everyone is not capable of going the easy way.

THE POWER OF SINLESSNESS

The brethren here are being prepared for the reconnection of the brain to the spinal cord. To stand up in full stature means that the full-grown man, Christ Jesus, will appear in you. That is what is being preached here. That is what we are waiting for, and that is what we are hoping for. When the full man Christ Jesus is reconnected in me and in you, it means full power over all the evil powers in the earth.

When that happens, the power is not just for us. We are in the army of God. We are responsible to find out what the Lord wants us to do with the power. The power of God is power over life and death in a world that is falling apart. Each of us will receive our specific assignment from the Lord.

Jesus' had power over nature, power over gravity, and power over life and death in the days of flesh. He raised the dead. We are waiting for a similar experience. The Lord will stand on the earth (incarnate) again in full spiritual power, and this time it will be in more than one person. There are going to be many sons of God with full power and authority over all the powers that rule over all of the world, not just the Church. The Government of God is coming to the earth. I do not honestly know how it is going to play out, but all these rogue nations with atom bombs will be dealt with.

The whole world is spiritually female right now, and the spiritual males that are here are very young. I believe there is spiritual manhood in this ministry, but it is very young. Christ cannot stop Iran from making an atomic bomb, He is very young. Another way of saying that He is very young is to say that He is only half a man, because He is not attached to His head yet. All power is in the head, the Lord Jesus Christ.

The whole world is at stake here. We are not here just listening to a message. We are here to have Christ built up in us, and when He is built up in us, He will overcome our carnal mind and appear in us (1 Jn 3:2).

SUBMISSION TO THE PASTOR

Listening to my messages will not help if you are in a conflict or a power play with the pastor You cannot r e j e c t t h e messenger and benefit from the messages unless you are judging your own soul. On the other hand, you are in danger of developing into a poisonous dragon like the female disciple in the movie, ***Crouching Tiger, Hidden Dragon.*** Listening to the messages while engaging in an ungodly relationship with the pastor will result in the negative consequence of becoming a spiritually powerful person on the evil side.

GOD'S GOVERNMENT

We are, spiritually speaking, a very, very, important ministry of God. I am not saying this to exalt ***LEM***. I am merely acknowledging God in this teaching. We are God's court and He is doing great things here. I do not know of any other ministry where God holds court. If He is doing it elsewhere, those ministries are far and few between and I do not know about them.

God holds court and decrees go forth from the spiritual ministry that He raises up here because His government. Is in His people. I am not taking any personal glory. I am asking you to see what Christ Jesus is doing here, and the high level of it. God held court when He revealed himself through the nation of Israel, and Solomon was His greatest judge. We may be among the first New Testament ministries where God holds court.

God is a troublemaker. He creates controversies (1 Ki 18:17) to help the personality escape when Christ falls down under the authority of the carnal mind. The personality that truly wants Christ escapes, but the personality that prefers its evil inclination, does not escape. Conflict distinguishes the two sides: The righteous side, and the unrighteous side.

TIME FOR ASCENSION

Brethren, we do not ascend because we are cute little children, or because the Lord likes the way we smile. This is a serious business. We do not ascend until we pass the test, and overcoming the warfare with the evil inclination is a part of the test! The ascension is happening so the test comes to all of us eventually. I am not trying to frighten you. It is exciting, but our mind has to be in the right place to ascend.

We climb the spiritual ladder (Gen 28;12) into ascension. We do not get a gold star when we ascend. We climb up. Every step up is an overcoming of an aspect of our carnal mind which involves identifying and condemning ungodly motives and behavior. I am speaking to you from the Mind of God. I have no power to cause you to ascend or to not ascend. I am God's mouthpiece, and I am speaking the Word of the Lord. If you want to ascend, you must identify and condemn ungodly motives and behavior.

A son of God is not a dress or suit that we put on that says *son of God.* Either we think and do what a son of God thinks and does, or we do not. It is not possible to have wrong thinking and a righteous motive at the same time. A wrong motive makes us a natural man and not a son of God in that situation. No matter how high we ascend, we will not be able to stay up there if we bring our carnal mind up with us. we will surely fall down again

HONOR AND INTEGRITY

God's Army

God is raising up an army of righteous men (I use that term ***men*** generically). There is an honor code at Annapolis or West Point that requires officers of the United States military to be honorable men, gentleman. One lie and a cadet is out. Their education at Annapolis or West Point is finished and their career in the United States military is finished. It is not honorable to lie. Lying is a character flaw that God expects every son of God to overcome. We cannot play games with God. This is a serious business. The whole world is at stake.

We have two sides. When our evil side overtakes us, we become Judas. Brethren, we all manifest our evil side from time to time, and some of us manifest more than others. Brethren manifesting character flaws should not be condemned and we never know when our ***day of calamity*** will arrive. No one knows what ungodly behavior or attitudes they will manifest when they are tested.

We are the chameleon. One minute we are Christ and the next minute we are the Devil opposing God's work. Our carnal mind rises to the surface and attacks when we let go of Christ.

Each of us is a personality, a mask that hides spiritual life. One day, or one minute, it can be Christ speaking through us, and the next day, or next minute, it can be pride. We cannot judge by what we see or hear with these eyes and ears.

Isaiah 11:3
³ AND SHALL MAKE HIM OF QUICK UNDERSTANDING IN THE FEAR OF THE LORD: AND HE SHALL NOT JUDGE

AFTER THE SIGHT OF HIS EYES, NEITHER REPROVE AFTER THE
HEARING OF HIS EARS: **KJV**

We cannot judge by what we see or hear with these eyes
and ears, because these eyes and ears see only the personality,
which is a mask. It is false; it is a lie. We have to see what is
inside the person.

The only survivors of a spiritual war are the people
who are spiritual. Have integrity, do not lie, be honorable. If
you have to defend yourself, just tell the truth. If you make a
mistake or do something wrong, say you are sorry.

The Lord wants us to ascend and we ascend through
change. All of us are unrighteous. All have sinned and have
fallen short of the glory of God.

Romans 3:23
²³ FOR ALL HAVE SINNED, AND COME SHORT OF THE
GLORY OF GOD; **KJV**

We ascend by overcoming unrighteousness, as the
Lord leads us. If you do not know what area of unrighteousness
the Lord is working with you on at the moment, ask Him. Ask
Him how you can improve, how you can acquire more
integrity. There is always repentance.

OUR CHARACTER IS US

This is a positive message. Unrighteousness cannot be dealt with until it is exposed, so all unrighteousness must be exposed. We have to see it. We have to look at ourselves and see those ugly blemishes. Then the Lord will work with us to make ourselves beautiful. We can go the easy way or the hard way, but the only way to ascend is through the exposure of sin. Character is number one, because our character reveals whether we are Christ or the fallen man. Supernatural signs and wonders are not signs of righteousness. These are gifts given to the repentant and unrepentant alike. Satan does supernatural signs and wonders.

Some people have character and other people do not, but it is your character, brethren, that reveals who you are. Years ago, when I was a young disciple, I was in a deliverance church. One day I asked the Lord how we will know if Christ has risen in us. Will we have power to deliver people, to cast out demons? The Lord said, *No, these are not the signs of Christ's presence,* but He did not tell me what the sign was. It has taken all of these years for me to understand that the sign of Christ's presence is character, brethren, and not just on the surface, but on the inside. Character in your inward part does not falter when the wind blows, so it is fiery trials that distinguish between what is on the surface and what is on the inside – between what is real, and what is false.

I have been on this journey for a long time. I am not in any way perfect, but I have taken a lot of victories and changed a lot. I am speaking to you from experience. God will put character in our inward part if we are willing to pay the price (Ps 51:6). *We need to face our weaknesses, and hate them.*

If we see a weakness in ourselves and want God to change us, we must want that change badly enough to do whatever it takes. We cannot say, *I see pride in myself, and I want to ascend, so please get rid of it for me.* No. We must hate that thing, or that behavior. We must see it. Maybe no one else is seeing it, but we must know what is in our own heart.

We must hate being that way. Sometimes, it takes a long time for Him to change us, but we must continue to hate it, resist it, deny it, punish that quality in ourselves, whatever it is. Bind it up, rebuke it, and ask God to replace it with its righteous counterpart. That is how we climb by the spiritual power of Christ Jesus that overcomes sin. We do not climb by knowledge of doctrine. We climb by what we do, how we relate to other people, and how we fight this spiritual warfare. We climb by recognizing what is not of God in ourselves and putting it on the altar to be burnt up. We must kill whatever is in us that offends us (Matt 5:30), not what offends us in the other person.

CLEAVING TO GOD THROUGH RIGHTEOUSNESS

We must prosper if we stand with righteousness, no matter what the problem is. If it is our health, if we are ill, if we have emotional problems, if we have financial problems, whatever our problem is, we must prosper when we cleave to righteousness. We might not see the results that we are looking for right away, because God is building that righteousness in us. Sometimes we have to struggle for righteousness to come forth in us. And sometimes we do not understand His ways. But if you cleave to righteousness, nothing, nothing, can take you out. Nothing, nothing, can destroy you.

We must cleave to our God, and the only way to cleave to Him is through the righteousness that is inside of us, not through doctrine. We will not be blown over when wo what is right and! The winds are blowing, brethren; it is getting tough out there. Everything that can be shaken is being shaken. This means that there will be hard times, times that we will need to be close to our God to have our needs met. The winds are blowing

Embrace the trial! Pressure makes us vulnerable to sin, so we ask the Lord to give us the victory when we are under that pressure. We embrace the trial by asking the Lord to help us get through it without sin. The judgments are going to intensify as the appearance of Christ Jesus in His fullness gets closer. The pressure is going to intensify, and it is Satan and Leviathan, our fallen nature, who are hysterical, because Christ is about to stand up in us and destroy them.

What does *stand up* mean? It is a misnomer to say *He is about to stand up*. The Scripture says that *on that day His feet will stand on t h e Mount o f Olives*. The Lord has shown us that the Mount of Olives is in the brain stem. Christ Jesus is rising up from within us, because the spiritual worlds are within us. The Lord Jesus above is about to join with Christ in the earth, which is us.

Abel, that drop of the supernal world that is under the dominion of the carnal mind, is being awakened, quickened, and developed. He is like a flower opening up, but his power is limited because he is disconnected from the supernal worlds. The Lord Jesus is coming down, literally descending into us, and joining with Christ in our brain. He is reconnecting us to the supernal worlds, to impart the ability to be fully righteous, the requirement for immortality, because our ability to be righteous is limited without Him.

When we live a righteous life, no accuser that can prevail over us. If we are sick, an accuser has prevailed over us. If we lose our wealth, an accuser has prevailed over us. The Sowing & Reaping Judgment has declared us guilty, and our sin has not yet been fully forgiven.

The union of the head, the Lord Jesus Christ, to Christ, His relative in our body, is the complete defense against all decrees, through the impartation of Christ's perfect righteousness to us. We need to develop as much righteousness as we can in preparation for the union of Christ within us with the ultimate righteousness, which imparts His immortal life to us.

Brethren, this doctrine produces spiritual ascension. Jesus said, ***Let the wheat and the tares grow together*** (Matt 143:30) This means that the evil side grows, and the good side grows. It is a continuous warfare between good and evil within the individual, until the Lord Jesus Christ joins himself to our good side and overcomes the evil side completely. The Lord Jesus Christ, who has complete authority over all power and principalities (Col 2:10), strengthens Christ within us. Cain within us is strengthened by Satan and Leviathan. It is the

34

collective Christ in this ministry fighting with those powers and principalities on behalf of those of us who cannot fight for themselves.

TABLE OF REFERENCES

ABOUT THE AUTHOR

Sheila R. Vitale is the Spiritual Leader, Founding Teacher, and Pastor of *Living Epistles Ministries (LEM)*. She moves in the offices of Teacher of Apostolic Doctrine, Prophet, Evangelist and Pastor, has an international following, and has been expounding on the Scripture through a unique spiritual lens for nearly three decades.

She has written more than 50 books based on the Old and New Testaments including *Ephraim, Man of the Earth and The Eagle Ascended (OT), and Salvation* and *Not Without Blood (NT)*. She has also rendered original spiritual interpretations of Biblical texts such as *The Woman in The Well (John, Chapter 4)* and *First Corinthians, Chapter 11*. Her unique, Multi-Part Message style is seen in *LEM* Serial Messages such as *A Place Teeming With Life* (9 Parts) and *Quantum Mechanics in Creation* (18 Parts). Each Part of a Multi-Part Message Series can also be enjoyed as a complete and independent study. In addition, she has defined, explained, illustrated and demonstrated hundreds of spiritual principles throughout more than 1,000 *LEM* Lectures.

Her signature work, however, is the three volumes of *The Alternate Translation Bible (ATB)*: *The Alternate Translation of The Old Testament*, *The Alternate Translation of The New Testament* and *The Alternate Translation of the Book of Revelation*. *The Alternate Translation Bible* is a work in progress (*The ATB Project*). Accordingly, additional spiritual interpretations of both whole and partial Chapters are added from time to time, as they are rendered. The most up-to-date versions of *The ATB Project* may be found online at *The LEM* Website (*LivingEpistles.org*). *The ATB* is a *spiritual interpretation* of the Scripture and is not intended to replace traditional translations.

She also analyzed the Greek text of *The Book of Revelation* and preached extensively on it in the early years of *The ATB Project*. During that time she produced 197 distinct *Message Parts*, under 29 specific *Message Titles*, all of which deal with *The Book of*

Revelation. Also, many of her books such as, *Adam and The Two Judgment*s and *A Study in Unconscious Mind Control*, have been translated into Spanish, as well as *The Book of Revelation.*

Pastor Vitale is an illustrator of spiritual principles, a researcher, a translator and a reviewer of the Modern Social Trends of Family and Culture, as they are revealed through TV programs (*The Sopranos),* movies (*The Matrix* and *The Edge of Tomorrow)* and plays (*Wicked*). She also writes for the *LEM Blog.*

She travels domestically, as well as internationally, preaching and teaching Judeo-Christian Spiritual Philosophy, and has donated Audio Libraries of her Lectures to other ministries in Africa, Asia, Europe and North America,

Pastor Vitale serves *LEM* in a range of spiritual, educational, and administrative functions from *The Selden Centre, LEM* headquarters in Selden, New York. She is also a philanthropic individual who supports the *Lighthouse Mission (Patchogue, NY) and HGM − Mission of Hope − Haiti, and other* charitable organizations. She also supports community services such as the *Terryville Fire Department.*

In her spare time, Pastor Vitale enjoys watching movies, attending plays and partaking of cuisines from different cultures. An avid traveler, she has visited several countries in Europe and Africa as well as many cities in the United States.

BEGINNINGS, INSPIRATION AND CALLING

Pastor Vitale began her spiritual journey as a child when her Jewish mother enrolled her in the Hebrew school of an Orthodox synagogue. She experienced the Spirit of God for the first time there in such a profound way that she wept. But after that, when she was only eleven years old, she became very ill and was taken to Mount Sinai Hospital in New York City. She almost died there and has battled with life-threatening health issues ever since. Nevertheless, a deep longing for God continued to pursue her until several years later when she desperately wanted to attend Yeshiva (Jewish high school), but could not. Her secular parents approved of her choice, but could not afford the tuition.

Much later, after years of searching, she once again experienced the Spirit that had brought her to tears in the synagogue of her youth, but this time it was at *Gospel Revivals Ministries*, a Pentecostal church where Deliverance Ministry was emphasized. She had a desire to understand the Bible since she was a child, but Scripture was difficult for her and she struggled with the text. Nevertheless, she read one Chapter of the Bible every day until, one day, *her spiritual eyes opened* and she saw an angel holding a little book.

After that, she attended as many as five teaching services each week for about seven years, the latter part of which she edited *Pastor Holzhauser's* books. But several more years had to pass before *the eyes of her understanding opened even further* and she began to receive *Revelation Knowledge of the Scripture*. She understood at that time that the angel she had seen was the angel of Revelation 10:8.

After about seven years of learning *Deliverance Ministry* and *The Doctrine of Sonship* (*Bill Britton*) from *Pastor Holzhauser,* she studied the Bible independently under the influence and direction of the Holy Spirit.

In **1998** she began teaching Apostolic Doctrine.

In **1990** she spent three months in Stony Brook Hospital where she recovered from an incurable disease, defeating premature death, once again, and went on to resume teaching and managing *LEM*.

In **1992** she journeyed to Africa for the first time, where she was called to the office of Evangelist.

In the **mid-1990s,** she began to Pastor in addition to being a Teacher of Apostolic Doctrine, a Prophet and an Evangelist, thus, satisfying all five offices of *The Ministry of the Lord Jesus Christ to*

His Church.

LIVING EPISTLES MINISTRIES

Pastor Vitale was happy fellowshipping at *Gospel Revivals Ministries* but, eventually, she desired a deeper and more spiritual understanding of the Word of God. One day, after crying out to Jesus about her need, she was amazed to hear Him ask her if she would teach. Her initial response was that she did not see how it would be possible since she was already working a full-time job, despite her poor health. But after the Lord asked her for a second and then a third time, she reluctantly agreed, believing that He would empower her to do the job. Shortly thereafter, in the latter part of 1987, she began to teach her own brand of Judeo-Christian Spiritual Philosophy.

The Lord Jesus Christ named the work *Living Epistles Ministries* in 1988.

The first *LEM* meetings were casual and spontaneous gatherings of friends and fellow deliverance workers in Pastor Vitale's home. After that, they were held in the business office of one of the brethren. Pastor Vitale delivered her first formal message entitled *The Truth About Witchcraft in January of 1988*, followed by *The Seduction of Eve* in April of the same year. After that, she prepared and taught weekly messages including *Signs of Apostleship* and *Lazarus & The Rich Man. The meetings eventually* increased to two and then three each week.

Sometime after that, she learned that the Lord Jesus Christ was revealing spiritual principles from the Hebrew text of the Old Testament through her teachings, and she used those spiritual principles to begin to unlock the mysteries of the New Testament, as well. Today she understands that the Scripture is a spiritual document that must be spiritually discerned if it is to be understood correctly, and calls that spiritual understanding ***The Doctrine of Christ***.

LEM publishes a wide range of material, including books, e-books, spiritual interpretations of the Scripture and transcripts of many of Pastor Vitale's Lectures and on-line meetings, all of which, as well as the entire *Alternate Translation Bible,* may be viewed free of charge on the *LEM* website (*LivingEpistles.org*). She also has an *Author's Website* where all of her books, as well as several photographs of herself and a short biography are displayed (Amazon.com/author/SheilaVitale). Paperback and digital versions of *LEM* books may be purchased through *Amazon*, *Google Books* and *Barnes & Noble.*

LEM provides free video livestreams through YouTube and other Internet Platforms . . .

@LivingEpistlesMinistries (2016 – Sept. 2022)
@LivingEpistlesMinistriesLEM (Oct. 2022 – Ongoing)
@LivingEpistlesMinistries (LEM disciples)

. . . as well as two channels of **Shortclips** where short, focused messages of about 15 minutes each are posted:

@shortclipsbysheilar.vitale3334 (2016 – Sept. 2022)
@ShortClips-SheilaVitale (Oct. 2022 – Ongoing)

LEM donates a significant percentage of its income to other Christian ministries and organizations that advocate for Christian values and defend the United States Constitution.

PASTOR VITALE TODAY

Today Pastor Vitale continues to dedicate her life to teaching the spiritual principles of the Bible and focuses daily on studying, writing and preaching powerful messages from *The Selden Centre,* LEM/CCK's headquarters at Selden, New York.

ADAM & THE TWO JUDGMENTS

Sheila R. Vitale – Living Epistles Ministries

Living Epistles Ministries
Sheila R. Vitale
Pastor, Teacher & Founder
Judeo-Christian Spiritual Philosophy
PO Box 562, Port Jefferson Station, New York 11776, USA
LivingEpistles.org
or
Books@LivingEpistles.org

www.ingramcontent.com/pod-product-compliance
Lightning Source LLC
LaVergne TN
LVHW051817080426
835513LV00017B/1988

* 9 7 8 0 6 9 2 4 0 2 6 7 2 *